THE CAVE

Tom Holmes

BITTER OLEANDER
P R E S S

The Bitter Oleander Press
4983 Tall Oaks Drive
Fayetteville, New York 13066-9776 USA

www.bitteroleander.com
info@bitteroleander.com

Copyright © 2014 by Tom Holmes

ISBN 10: 09883525-2-4
ISBN 13: 978-0-9883525-6-8

Library of Congress Control Number: 2014949112

Layout & Design: Roderick Martinez
Cover photograph: "Skull Tracks" by Paul B. Roth

Printed by McNaughton & Gunn, Inc.
Saline, Michigan 48176-0010
www.bookprinters.com

Distributed in the United States by Small Press Distribution, Inc.
Berkeley, CA 94710-1409
www.spdbooks.org

Manufactured in the United States of America

ACKNOWLEDGMENTS

These poems, or versions of them, first appeared in the following journals:

Artifact Literary Journal: "The Phases of Sharpening a Blade"; "Contacting the Dead"
The Adroit Journal: "The Invention of Tattoos"
Blood Lotus Journal: "The Cap Blanc Girl's Last Thoughts"
Boston Literary Magazine: "The Mind in the Sky"
The Camroc Press Review: "When the Sun Is Angry" (previously "The Ancient Art of Carrying Anger")
The Chaffey Review: "A Brief Autobiography of the First Artist"
Clockhouse Review: "The Needle"
East Coast Literary Review: "Fireside"
The Flagler Review: "The Birth of Knowledge"
The Foundling Review: "The Gasp"
The Fourth River: "The First Songs – Archaboilus Musicus' Songs from the Mid-Jurassic"
Heron Tree: "The Invention of Inspiration"
Journal of Kentucky Studies: "The Creation of a Hearth"; "Fire"
Knockout Literary Magazine: "Paleolithic Person on the Burial of Art"
Le Mot Juste: "Songs in Altamira"
Miramar: "The World Is Not"; "Paleolithic Person Describes Dreaming"
Naugatuck River Review: "The Carver of the 'Mal'ta Venus' Reflects on the Figurine"
North American Review: "The Shell Girl"
The North Chicago Review: "The Invention of the Doll"
OVS Magazine: "Dinner Time in the Paleolithic"
Pebble Lake Review: "Paleolithic Person Tells of the Invention of Harmony and Melody"
Poetry Quarterly: "The Invention of the Ellipsis"; "Paleolithic Person Discovers Fear"
The Portland Review: "Paleolithic Person Explains Cave Art and the Apocalypse"; "The Appearance of Symbolism and Metaphor"
Rock & Sling: "Paleolithic Person Explains Why He Paints Deep in the Cave"; "Paleolithic Person Explains Hand Art"; "The Afterlife of the First Dreams"; "The First Prayer"; "An Origin of the Other"
The Round: "Flower Burial"; "Paleolithic Person on the Burial of the Dead"
Santa Clara Review: "Paleolithic Person Explains Her Footprints"
The Sierra Nevada Review: "The Double Venus of Grimaldi"
Silk Road Review: "Paleolithic Possession"; "Paleolithic Person Learns to Sing"
Southern Humanities Review: "The First Potter's Advice"
The Stone Highway Review: "The First Painting"
Three Line Poetry: "Remnants of the First Sad Story"
Turbulence: "What They Saw in the Afterlife"

"The Invention of the Doll," "The First Prayer," and "Paleolithic Person Explains Cave Art and the Apocalypse" were 2012 Pushcart Prize nominees.

CONTENTS

CAVE ARTS

THE INVENTIONS OF SONG AND DANCE

THE FEASTS

SECULAR LIVES

THE OTHER SIDE OF THE WALL

THE CAVE

For
Charles Mingus' *Pithecanthropus Erectus*
and
Sibelius' *Finlandia, Legends, Valse Triste, The Oceanides*, and *Tapiola*
and
My Parents
and
Sophie

CAVE ARTS

PALEOLITHIC PERSON EXPLAINS WHY HE PAINTS DEEP IN THE CAVE

When my brother could no longer hunt,
when he could no longer protect the food,
when he could no longer plant the seed,
I knew he would become the ground.

I feared he would be lost and alone,
so I sprayed a trail of dots
from the cave's mouth, along the walls,
stalagmites, stalactites, the ceiling,
and all the way to sanctuary.

I set down my bowl of burning animal fat
to illuminate this hollow of the world.

With a beaver's tail and colored pigments,
I painted pictures of horses and spears
to amaze him as he settled through the earth.

For his partner, who would have to beg
for flesh, who would starve herself alone,
who would soon follow my brother's passage,
for her I carved the bison with the wound.

PALEOLITHIC PERSON EXPLAINS HAND ART

A meteor breaks through the sky.
It blazes a tail like a bison's
before it mounts or fights,
then arcs, falls, and dissolves.

There's a crack in the cave wall,
propped open with bone slivers,
where you can hear the dead whisper
and feel their cold breaths.

Tonight they're quiet
and listen to the meteor whistle
a song it carries from a star.
Hearing from other worlds is rhapsodic.

When I put my fingertips to the crack
and blow black paint around and on my hand
I melt through to the other side.
I go often. Tonight I'll catch the meteor's song.
If I don't return, look for the ghost of my palm.

THE INVENTION OF INSPIRATION

This time as the sun sets
I crawl to the cave's lowest level.
Howls and whispers roll by.
I'm an ear in the cave.

Down here, the sun is a deep pond,
and I'm a diaphanous shadow –
the air tastes good to my palate,
and the slow colors rise in me.

Beasts leap from my hands.
I may never return.

THE MIND IN THE CAVE

I press my eyes and see three moons.
If my eyes tear, I see six or nine.
Down here the wind is cold.

When drums find their rhythm
with flames and dancers,
the cracks in the walls spray light.

When the wall sees through me
with eyesight as strong as the moon,
I'm a shadow in night sky.

When the wall opens,
I am lightning in the antelope's antlers
and the stripe along its jaw.

If I return, you'll hear me
cackle my way from the other side
and paint what's in a mind.

THE FIRST PAINTING

I had no urge except to sleep
with her in the cave, but I felt
sympathy. I cared. I sensed
intelligence in a crevice. I saw

life. I saw a bison's back
in a crack. I saw
the whole world, the whole sky,
all of night. The night

was alive, here, underground
with the bisons, the horses, and rhinos
before me, before my eyes – I saw
a backdrop with all the beasts.

I saw blood on my finger.
The arc of a bison's back
appeared with one stroke.
The second urge arrived.

PALEOLITHIC POSSESSION

My paint brush is made of hair
plucked from a dead beaver's ear.

The wind blows through the cave,
its growls and whines fill every hollow.

When my brush is dry,
I see where the wind has been –

my painting is not of the bison
but of where the wind took form.

THE APPEARANCE OF SYMBOLISM AND METAPHOR

And as we rise from crawling
to the end of the cave,

our paintings transform into meanings,
the images work out *Sex* and *Death* –

all the sienna bison
huddle on the wall

each with one eye open.
We with paint on our hands.

THE FIRST POTTER'S ADVICE

When sculpting a lion's head,
your fingers should stroke the neck
and caress its clay mane.
Its eyes should reflect yours.

If you rub too eagerly
and the head falls to your feet,
you can hollow its skull
and fill it with seeds.

If the eyes are dull
like your clay covered fingerprints,
it's best to bend it to a turtle's shell
and fill it with water and hot stones.

If the mane starts to curl
like a hawk's talons
before it flies, bite your tongue,
and push the lion to the hearth.

Or should I say, to shape a lump of clay
is to hear children in the sea
leaping, splashing, and yelling –
there is no containing them.

THE INVENTION OF THE ELLIPSIS

She dreams of hogs
with rotten teeth
and brusque growls.
She dreams of their meat.

By a stone lamp
of burning hog marrow,
she kneels and twists hog hairs
and ties them to a rib bone.

She drags the bristles
through yellow and black pigments,
dabs a stream of dots,
and paints her other dreams.

THE AFTERLIFE OF THE FIRST DREAMS

Her dreams appeared in the cave.
The deeper she slept,
the more startling the paintings arrived.

When she awoke, she beheld
her dreams
leaping from wall to wall.

The fire collapsed.
Darkness settled in like a new moon
through a cloudy night.

She picked up burnt wood and ash
and drew shadows
like a grave under her dreams
or a tunnel to waking.

THE DOUBLE VENUS OF GRIMALDI

her head her head
                    unfolds unfolds
            into its badger eyes
and out its yellow mouth
and when she breathes
            she once inhales a breath
                    which circles round
                            and out its badger mouth
                    and when she sleeps
            she wakes a dream
that is a memory
            waking in discrete

                    could she spin
            should she spin
in the wind or in the breeze
            and twist or twirl
                    around a woman's neck
                            she'll dream a sleep
                    as long as her last
            good bye good bye
and in the end
            and in the end
                    a yellow strand of serpentine
            bends and bends
into her face
            with no eye no eye
                    the dread of forgetting
            and nothing to identify

THE INVENTIONS
OF
SONG AND DANCE

THE FIRST SONGS – ARCHABOILUS MUSICUS' SONGS FROM THE MID-JURASSIC

In the thin forest night, the katydids rise.
They wake. They start to sing.
Ferns drip from the afternoon rain,
the stream babbles to the waterfall,
and reptiles and amphibians dream.

Some dream serenely, some irritably
as if for the first time they heard of love.
They focus themselves to listen and to locate.
They listen like a concert audience backstage
anticipating how and where the melody ends.

The katydids' songs chime as wide as the wild woods.
The pine trees and fir trees grow a little more.
The needles' colors brighten as if about to flame.
How unrestrained the melodies are
that drift over predators and to their possible mates.

Their songs spark images in the loved and the hungry.
If I were there, I'd hear them in my dreams,
and when I awoke with their last notes at twilight,
I'd find a cave or a tree and begin to paint or carve,
while the katydids returned to their hiding and composing.

THE GASP

I hold my breath and run
and the tighter I hold
the faster I go
or I paint the wind
across an auroch's back
and around its horns
with one interminable stroke

The exhale is arrival or awe
unless you have a flute
then it's announcement
of where you've been

Inhale is energy
and the beginning of dance
which is music
which are sounds running together
until they drop to the dirt

I must keep busy
else I'll sleep
away the days
in the awe of dirt

PALEOLITHIC PERSON EXPLAINS HER FOOTPRINTS

I needed something to burn,
something to light this hollow of the cave,
something to warm me against the wind,
I was sucking marrow from a bone.

Exhale and suck. Exhale and suck.
Exhale and the sound of gloom from the bone.
Exhale and the sound of a bison
before it mounts its mate.

The moan pulsed in my ear
like the drowsiness of wind at night.
I exhaled and blew over and over.
My hands were trembling.

Exhale and suck. Exhale and suck.
The empty bone. Tones deeper
than the sound of settling ash.
I wished for a higher sound. A sound of joy.

I thought to give the bone ears to hear,
I thought to give the bone a mouth to breathe,
I carved into its side a hole
and then another and another.

I had invented the hole.
I covered the holes with my fingers
and invented graves for my breaths.
I had invented burial.

I lifted a finger to release one breath
like an ember rising in the wind.
I invented the high sound.
I invented the long breath and the short.

My eyes widened as I heard what I played,
my ears focused on breathing and pattern,
my fingers bounced up and down,
my fingers invented dancing.

My legs followed my fingers in the dance.
My feet charted this joy of rhythm in the dirt.
I forgot the holes and the graves. I breathed with ease.
I invented distraction from dying.

PALEOLITHIC PERSON LEARNS TO SING

Today I've learned to sing
the high voice of joy,
the color of green,
the arms stretching to the sun,
the leaping deer,
the floating ember,
the rising.

The winter, however, doesn't end
with the bloom of a lily.
The snow falls
but not like the rain,
but dried leaves
rising from the ground
with a gust of wind.

How do I sing it? –
the joy of the end?
How do I greet the dead?
I'm a painter.
I paint for all who'll die.
These notes are new.
How do I sing to the dead?

If I were a fire,
I'd melt all the snow
to raise the dead
like blooming lilies.
I am not fire,
but I have memories
of blowing and the first flame rising.
Tonight I will sing
to you, the dead, an elegy,
until you arrive
from a womb
crying in tune
with the color of joy,
the arms rising for life.

PALEOLITHIC PERSON TELLS OF THE INVENTION OF HARMONY AND MELODY

In the middle of winter,
I blew into my hands
for warmth. I thought of the Neanderthal
in spring with a blade of grass
between his fingers
blowing out a harmony
with spring, grass, and his humanity.

I wrapped my hands like this
with my thumbs slightly split.
I blew like the Neanderthal
but more graceful, like an owl
at night sighting a mouse
over its shoulder then letting it go
just to hear its own owl song.

SONGS IN ALTAMIRA

Nothing in my cave escapes –
the image of rolling bison,
the sympathies of the reindeer,
the high view from the horse's head,
not even the leaping boar
or its grunts or growls.

Nothing in my cave escapes –
I echo with paintings each beast
that ever has lived. Go ahead sing.
The animals are attentive.
They will listen as always
to all the songs ever sung.

Songs make for living, so sing
something new. Make the beasts strut,
make them dance along the walls,
make a memory of sympathy,
make them live once more as if outside –
nothing in my cave will ever escape.

THE FEASTS

THE FIRST PRAYER

Father, it is cold for spring,
snow lingers in shadows
below cliffs and trees,
the ground is not giving,
and the beasts smell you.

The fat and dried meats
dwindled away days ago
as did your final breath.
The fire is warming.
Forgive us our next meal.

THE PHASES OF SHARPENING A BLADE

When sharpening flint,
use a full moon and strike.

The first cleaved flake is a crescent moon
and your prey has just been found.

A half moon is the blade you aim
to stab and carve your meals.

If you strike too fast or fierce
and flint shatters useless from your hand,

you're hunting with a new moon
and sleeping hungry in a tree.

THE CREATION OF A HEARTH

Begin by recruiting two cool firestones
from your grandmother's hearth.
Set one cornerstone here for her past,
and the other there for her tomorrows.

When the sun is prominent,
find yourself on a mountain's peak.
On your descent,
obtain the warmest rocks
from under the hooves of rams –
remember the shape of their toes.

You'll have the model
to arrange the rocks
from before and beyond
and make walls on the angled form.

When piled high as your knee,
fix a reindeer antler
to the corner of now.
As the hearth hardens,
pack mud into the cracks
and wait for fire.

FIRE

Smoke rises
through the hearth's cracks
like paintings
through a cave wall
or the dead
returning,

like flaring manure dollops
and mosquitoes fleeing,

like fires
stroking the high grass
and wolves
tracking flames

to sniff out cooked mice
and bobwhite quails
pecking charred grasshoppers,

I understand fire as paint –
it corrupts what it stains
and indicates life
once happened here.

DINNER TIME IN THE PALEOLITHIC

The hearth is a fixed sunset
in a tight chest.
                    Bright flames
contained by hunger and clay
murmur on a melting horizon
of meat and roots.

If this is my horizon,
I can lean into tomorrow,
incinerate the past,
or taste afterlives
of deer and tubers.
                    (The difference in distances
                        is the ability to digest
                        memory from the unknown.)

When the hearth glows
like the beginning of night,
ashes rise like insects
and fall like feathers
from a tree burdened by birds
settling in for the night.

If I rub my chest,
I can feel tomorrow
and its relaxed horizon
                    deliver a sun.

FIRESIDE

In dark, I have witnessed / time without pretense. – **Anon**

When time stops,
I forget to breathe

and hold my heartbeats
like a bowl of seeds.

The fire cracks
with cooked cicada skins.

The embers reflect
through tired moth eyes.

As time revives,
I gather those embers

and give them away –
presents of what may arrive,
an horizon suggesting light.

SECULAR LIVES

THE BIRTH OF KNOWLEDGE

As the wall cracked,
I hatched into your paint
and dilated pupils.

Then flowed into your world –
the world I'd witnessed
through a horse's eye.

It's dark here like screams
from the other side
but filled with ignorance.

When you invent red,
the screams will dissolve
like afterbirth in your teeth.

A BRIEF AUTOBIOGRAPHY OF THE FIRST ARTIST

I was carving
the sharp end of a spear
when I sliced myself
and my blood spilled out.

It was smooth and thick
and salty.
I tried to rub it off.
It spread evenly and thin.

More pulsed out
in rhythm with my heart.
I clutched my chest.
The blood continued its pulse.

I smeared my arm
and then my thigh.
I slapped a rock.
The blood held its place.

I found a red hand
on the rock. My red hand
detached and peaceful
like a greeting or foreboding.

My blood stopped.
I sliced myself again.
I made more hands
and flung red drops from my fingertips.

There was so much red
before it all went black.

PALEOLITHIC TIME

Today appears
like fire on a new moon –
the night falls like ash

THE MIND IN THE SKY

I look into night
the sky is dotted with stars –
it too will form beasts

THE SHELL GIRL

She collects drool
from a wounded deer
and stares into its eye
like she enters a cave.

She grinds drool into ochre.
When thick like sap,
when the mixing bone stands,
she dips a brush.

The cave wall opens
like a mollusk in fire,
she's a muscle the cave flexes,
her brush, an exposed nerve, swoops.

THE WORLD IS NOT

birds fall from the sky
antelopes roll them with their noses
if I were a hunter or gatherer
but rivers run from my toes
and fish gather in my palms
even when I dream

the world is not water or sky

two parts wood
one part dry grass
a mouthful of song
and fire curls tree leaves
around emptying stars
even when I believe

the world is not flora or fire

some seeds open with heat
others from soaking
either way my heart is the same
a thousand spiders crawl out
and spin one thousand webs
even when I imagine

the world is not without design

THE NEEDLE

Once I saw a spider weave a star
at sunrise, over extinguished embers
from the night's fire where we cooked
the deer we killed with our patience
and our spears.

          We scraped off its hide
and cut out its meat. We made food,
we made warmth, we were going to make clothes.

Let me tell you about the needle.
It is and it is not. It points
to what will be, and what it isn't
is in the eye. The eye where nothing is.
The nothing that pulls the thread.
The eye is the loop in a line. It is
the emptiness in the bone of the dead.
When I sharpen the bone, it is only a pin,
until I see to it that there is an eye –
the hook to pull the thread
of time.

          When we hunt, we're silent.
We don't speak or step on twigs.
We talk with our eyes and hands.

Eye of the needle.
Needle for the thread.

The long needle,
its eye
were once
alive
in the deer's
antlers,
a web
of antlers
with latent
needles.

The wind blew
through
the antler rack
like thread
through the eye.

Smooth needle,
long needle,
needle
puncturing through
the sides of hides.
Wild flax fiber threads
pull taut,
and the deer
reemerges
in a coat,
and the wind
blows around.
Blowing and blowing
around the hide,
down the hide,
until the hide cuts off
at the wrist,
then whips the knuckles
and the curve,
the space
between the fingers.
The wind blew harder,
and a flake of snow,
a flurry,
a snow fall
fell on the coat
and melted
like deer fat
in tonight's fire.

Needle like a tooth,
pine needle, beam of star light,
forgotten spider web
in tonight's fire,
melted.

Eye of the needle.
Needle for the thread.

A simple twist
of wild flax fiber
and the invention
of string,
and the twisting
of twisted threads
and strings
twists
into a rope,
and the deer
can be dragged
from the hunt
to the fire.

Eye of the needle.
Needle for the thread.

The needle is a spider
with wild flax fiber web,
a stitch, a weave,
an embroidery,
maker of shirts,
fabricator of pants,
form-fitting pants,
firm, warm pants
made supple from walking,
running, hunting,
smith of shoes,
the form of my feet
with soles,
the gloves, the hoods,
and articles of clothing
by article,
the embroidery
of warmth
with roots of pigments

to dye the flax
black, gray, pink,
violet, khaki, and green,
the birth of fashion,
a stitch in time,
the pattern, the style, the flow,
the figure,
my colors, my stitches,
my clan, my family,
my needle,
my place on earth –
a star in the sky.

Eye of the needle.
Needle for the thread.

THE INVENTION OF THE DOLL

Her first brother
wheezed and coughed.
She cradled him in her arms.

After his last breath,
she held on
to him for a month.

She petted him,
groomed him,
swatted off flies.

She carried her brother
over her back
until he mummified,

until grandmother
took him, laid him
on the river's current at night.

She watched in the sunrise
the wave roll
a small log to the bank.

She lifted the log,
stroked it, carried it home,
cradled it till the fire went out.

THE CAP BLANC GIRL'S LAST THOUGHTS

The horse bulges from the rock shelter wall
like a fetus trying to push a hand
through its mother's belly,
and I am the seminal cause of the creation.

That was before. Now there's a man
behind me with an ivory knife.
He pushes me down and slashes the air
in front of the horse's eye.

I crawl below its belly.
The man kneels and presses me down.
He looks to the horse's arching shoulder
and stabs me between the ribs.

The sun has warmed the dirt.
It comforts me between my long blinks.
Nothing has yet happened to the horse . . .
I've gone to the other side to push.

WHEN THE SUN IS ANGRY

I carry a flame
on a stick's end
to the black lake
at the bottom of the cave.

It's cool here
like the belly of the moon
on a clear night.
I reflect here.

I work the stick into the shore.
The fire burns at both ends.
The horses gallop across the walls
with bison and reindeer.

The fires meet and extinguish.
There's nothing but breathing
and odors of water and sunset.
The edge of the world is like this.

WHAT THEY SAW IN THE AFTERLIFE

They rubbed their eyes
then stared across fields
and up mountains
into a pale-blue sky.

Stones were struck.
Sparks leapt into fire.

A girl was spun and spun
until she fell
and raised questions
of an ungulate's missing teeth.

The breeze twisted her hair.
Her fingers unfurled.

The breadth of time
vanished like an open mouth
to an empty stomach
in an extinguished beast.

If only there were no eyes
to see what wasn't there.

THE OTHER SIDE OF THE WALL

Remnants of the first sad story –
a black bear's white teeth
and infant buried in a pit.

A NEANDERTHAL BURIAL RITUAL

Looking into a bison's skull
with no teeth
         is looking into night
Painting an eagle's talon toes
ochre red
       is learning to walk
Wearing a seal's skin
is scraping marrow
             from a heated bone
And burying your father
is all of this to him
           when he flies into the sun
Then you smash his spine
where it meets the head
scoop and eat his brains
and cover him
        with red flower petals

PALEOLITHIC PERSON ON THE BURIAL OF THE DEAD

With each scoop of earth,
I pile the dead's urges
and bake them in the sun.

I turn over the mounds
until the dirt is dry
enough to inhale or paint.

If I mix in red ochre,
the dead return as bulls.
With yellow, as horses.

If I mix in spit and manganese,
they will fly
into their next life.

If the dead trust my mixtures,
these genderless hands
will dig them another life.

If not, they'll decay into a memory
of ochre-stained bones
that no one will remember.

THE INVENTION OF TATTOOS

At night, sprinkle red ochre
on the recent dead.
In the morning, they'll return
and slaughter a herd of ibex or deer,
drain a river, or cloud the sky.

In the center of the cave,
they'll grow like calcite
or the echo of hot breath.

If you have a quartz pencil,
dip it in ochre paste
and draw half circles
under your eyes.

The dead will retire there
like a burial hole
and flood your mind
with memories
of where they've been.

FLOWER BURIAL

At the burial in the cave, a corpse
is wrapped with a red ochre stained shroud
in silence, and time begins
to revolve like echoed breathing.

Mortality and life intersect
as art of death and burial artist,
like brightly colored flowers
woven between a dead child's fingers.

From cornflower, hollyhock, and hyacinth,
pollen settles on the corpse
and on the floor. If pollen enters
the nose, the corpse revives

like an association revives the forgotten,
and deep within a cave's memory,
years hang like a stalactite
and the cure to forgetting drips.

The day the corpse is discovered,
with red ochre stained bones,
associations reassemble,
and someone inhales the pollen.

PALEOLITHIC PERSON DISCOVERS FEAR

Through the cave's mouth
the wind whistles
like a starling in spring.
All the way down here
with the pigment and bones
and a small fire,
the wind arrives
beaten and bruised,
the wind screams
as a nameless god
we haven't yet painted
or carved into the wall.

PALEOLITHIC PERSON ON THE BURIAL OF ART

The cave sleeps as the dead –
buried, reflective, and full of adornment.
What can be better
for them than art?

My beaver tail brush paints
with ghostly strokes and wisps
until the dawn arrives.
The images of the beasts grow and stalk.

What can be better for a hunt
than capturing the beasts
before they learn to cast a shadow?
Time on the wall slows as the dead.

PALEOLITHIC PERSON DESCRIBES DREAMING

I open the night
the moon scatters
like dandelion seeds

a foggy hand
gathers dampness
caresses my scalp

a dancer's voice flutters
as geese wings
glance along a lake

it is bright
as the glow of burning fat
behind me when I paint

so many dead
with nothing to offer
but the outlines of shadows

it is like staring into embers
the morning after fire
and trying to remember

CONTACTING THE DEAD

When birds die, they fall.
Big ones land loud on their bones.
Feathers lost in flight
can be plucked to aid in dreams
and to prepare a light meal.

Mute swans have long wings
and provide heavier meals.
Their long hollow bones
make good flutes for high-pitched songs
above ground or in caves.

Stalactites are teeth
or bones, and when struck, low tones
harmonize with bones
of flying, featherless birds –
the soul resides in all bones.

If you find a crack
in a cave wall, place a flute
in the hole and blow.
The fallen and dead listen
and return when you inhale.

THE CARVER OF THE "MAL'TA VENUS" REFLECTS

I carved his mother
from a mammoth tusk.
Then with an awl
pushed a hole through her feet.

I tied her likeness around his neck.
Her stubborn eyes
and listless mouth
looked up to him with regret.

Her folded ivory hands
smothered tragedy
as if to commence peace
or initiate a prayer.

There is always doubt
when you bury your child.
A statue like this did not remove it –
only burial and turning away did.

I carved his mother in the dress of the dead.
I walked away holding her hand
like we had time to fill
and a body to return to.

AN ORIGIN OF THE OTHER

And the air changed.
There had been wind and horizon,
fire and mammoths,
there were birds in the sky.
Where did all the voices come from?

And the ground changed.
Where did the ochre come from?
all the black manganese?
I crawl into the mouth of the cave.
I hear nothing but voices.

And the cave changed.
I draw what I remember,
I draw with black.
I paint so nothing dies,
I paint with red ochre.

And the voices changed.
Someone old talks to me
someone who became earth.
He talks from the wall
with the animals with the paint.

He talks of death
and the burial of the dead.
He talks of survival and the wall.
I am awed. I obey. I paint.
The past and future change.

NOTES, DEDICATIONS, & EPIGRAPHS

"The Invention of Inspiration" borrows a line from Walt Whitman

"Paleolithic Possession" is for Sarah Freligh

"The Appearance of Symbolism and Metaphor" is for Melissa Gioia

"The Afterlife of the First Dreams" is after Sergei Prokofiev's Symphony No. 3 in C Minor

"The First Songs – Archaboilus Musicus' Songs from the Mid-Jurassic." Archaboilus Musicus is a 165-million-year-old stridulating katydid from the Jurassic era. It provided a "paleoacoustic ecology." Its song was recently recreated by British scientists.

"The Cap Blanc Girl's Last Thoughts." The Cap Blanc Girl is a relatively intact skeleton from over 15,000 years ago that was found buried below a six-and-a-half foot horse frieze. She is one of the very few inhumations to be found near Paleolithic cave art.

"Paleolithic Person Discovers Fear" is for Donna Marbach

Special thanks to Thom Caraway for reading and finding homes for some poems, Steve Fellner for friendship and for reading an earlier version of the manuscript, Djelloul Marbrook for being awesome, William Heyen for suggesting the title of the book, Rob Carney whose rhythms and tones I often steal, Chris Howell and Jonathan Johnson for imaginative and compassionate inspiration, Angela Ball and Rebecca Morgan Frank for new energies, Laura McCullough and Christopher Buckley for spending time with this book, Alan Britt for reading and selecting this manuscript, Paul B. Roth for being delightful, for loving Caslon, and for being an editor who knows how to lay out a book of poems, and, of course, thanks to Melissa Gioia.

ABOUT THE AUTHOR

Tom Holmes is the editor of *Redactions: Poetry, Poetics, & Prose*. He is also author of *Poems for an Empty Church* (Palettes & Quills Press, 2011), *The Oldest Stone in the World* (Amsterdam Press, 2011), *Henri, Sophie, & the Hieratic Head of Ezra Pound: Poems Blasted from the Vortex* (BlazeVOX Books, 2009), *Pre-Dew Poems* (FootHills Publishing, 2008), *Negative Time* (Pudding House, 2007), *After Malagueña* (FootHills Publishing, 2005), and *Poetry Assignments: The Book* (Sage Hill Press, forthcoming). He has been nominated for the Pushcart Prize seven times, and his work has appeared a number of times on *Verse Daily*, as well as numerous journals. His current prose writing efforts about wine, poetry book reviews, and poetry can be found at his blog, *The Line Break: http://thelinebreak.wordpress.com/*.